YOUR KNOWLEDGE HAS VALUE

- We will publish your bachelor's and master's thesis, essays and papers

- Your own eBook and book - sold worldwide in all relevant shops

- Earn money with each sale

Upload your text at www.GRIN.com
and publish for free

Bibliographic information published by the German National Library:

The German National Library lists this publication in the National Bibliography; detailed bibliographic data are available on the Internet at http://dnb.dnb.de .

Imprint:

Copyright © 2017 GRIN Verlag
Print and binding: Books on Demand GmbH, Norderstedt Germany
ISBN: 9783346072030

This book at GRIN:

https://www.grin.com/document/505037

Christine Ndwiga

IT-Success. Moving From IT-Governance to Enterprise-Governance of Information Systems in Inter-Governmental Organisations

GRIN Verlag

GRIN - Your knowledge has value

Since its foundation in 1998, GRIN has specialized in publishing academic texts by students, college teachers and other academics as e-book and printed book. The website www.grin.com is an ideal platform for presenting term papers, final papers, scientific essays, dissertations and specialist books.

Visit us on the internet:

http://www.grin.com/

http://www.facebook.com/grincom

http://www.twitter.com/grin_com

IT Success;

Moving from just IT Governance to Enterprise Governance of Information Systems in Inter-Governmental Organisations

Christine Ndwiga

Masters Dissertation

Roehampton University

MSc. Information Systems Management

January 2017

Abstract

The way we utilise IT/IS has evolved. Frameworks are presently being utilised to kill monotonous undertakings and digitising prior work. Notwithstanding, another utilisation of IT/IS frameworks is installed in basic leadership and authoritative change. This development requests a higher speculation; it is no longer simply the PC or Server. Words like Value, Strategic Roadmap, IT Business Alignment, Integration, ERP and so on are being tossed around to focus an organisation's full potential. This drive for higher value accompanies a sticker price and risks. The research seeks to fill the gap by undertaking a comprehensive research of the success of IT governance and governance of IS in the intergovernmental organisations using a case-study of UNICEF Kenya. This study will fuse a scrutiny of already distributed papers on this subject and conclude deductions on IT/IS administration structures and methodologies that have been demonstrated to work for the new-age organisation by utilising the post-positivism philosophy and descriptive research design. The literature review of the study will demonstrate how intergovernmental organisations implement different levels of IS integration to improve their operations in the global arena. The literature also will highlight to a smaller extent some of the impacts of IT governance on intergovernmental organisations. The researcher utilised UNICEF Kenya for the sample selection of the study. The results of the research portray that IT governance and enterprise governance of IS have significance in improving the strategic planning or organisations. The findings of the study demonstrate that one of the major successes brought by the enterprise governance of information systems is the provision of enhanced strategic governance in the intergovernmental organisations. Consequently, the study outcomes have also portrayed some of the factors necessary for the success of IT governance in intergovernmental organisations.

- Need for the organisations to view IT as a strategic business asset and also to manage it as a significant portfolio.
- Discourage IT ignorance among the employees, and the IT staff contribute in technology investment resolutions.
- Need to have a vibrant IT executive and a board of director-level oversight
- The success of the IT governance is determined by the level in which these organisations perform monitoring and measurement.

Key Words: IT governance, IS governance, IS Integration, intergovernmental organisation, organisational performance.

List of Abbreviations

IT – Information Technology

IS – Information Systems

ITG- Information Technology Governance

PC- Personal Computer

ERP- Enterprise Resource Planning

HR- Human Resources

HRM - Human Resources Management

ISACA - Information Systems Audit and Control Association

FTEs - full-time employee equivalents

ITIL - Information technology infrastructure library

COBIT - Control Objectives for Information and Related Technologies

ASL - Application services library

CMM - The capability maturity model

Table of Contents

Chapter 1: Introduction

1.1 Background

Throughout the years, various top to bottom research about that focus on individuals, their connections, and states of mind to the inner and outer situations and pieces incorporating the progression and use of IT/IS structures have been conducted. The global integration of information systems by the intergovernmental organisations has triggered the emergence of certain trends that have a positive impact on the strategic governance of these organisations. In a submission by Ndwiga (2016, p.12;13), "Effective IT governance is vital for any organisation because it helps them to achieve their overall corporate governance. The corporate governance structure of any public sector organisation is sometimes 'very complex' so a lot of effort is required to 'achieve their organisational goal' (Biermann and Boas, 2010, p.66). It also provides some effective solutions regarding strategic issues (Scherer and Palazzo, 2011, p.900)". Ndwiga (2016, p.14;15) continues to state that "According to the current trends, technological advancements help different organisations to improve their services. Effective corporate governance can assist mitigate risks anticipated in business conducted. However, it is a little bit difficult for any organisation to maintain their total corporate governance principles like the role of their board, auditing, the quality related to their financial reporting, remuneration of the director, etc. It is not possible to manage all of the principles of corporate governance without a proven framework. An IT framework is applied this way (Hirst, 2013, p.17). As stated by Pollitt and Bouckaert (2011, p.62), execution of an Enterprise governance framework utilising IT is truly troublesome for any non-IT organisation. This is because, where the corporate governance structure is very complex like in most public sector organisations, there are potential outcomes that the IT system may fall flat at the initial stage. Alongside that, IT administration systems may flop in the operation level since it requires an extraordinary skill set and research has demonstrated that public sector employees might not have the required IT skill (Armitage et al. 2010, p.75)". Ndwiga (2016) concludes that "There may also be challenges in collating the right team to the project as inter-governmental organisations may have a geographic spread".

1.2 Research Aims and Objectives

The study will dwell on two general aims that include:

- To investigate the influence of IT governance on the performance of intergovernmental organisations
- To evaluate how intergovernmental organisations can implement enterprise governance of information systems to enhance their output

The objectives of the research include:

- To critically provide a literature review of the basic constructs of the study, that is, the impact of the IT governance and the enterprise governance of information systems in different intergovernmental organisations. The literature review will evaluate the ways of transforming IT governance into enterprise governance of information systems in intergovernmental organisations. Consequently, the review will also highlight the different levels of integration of information systems in intergovernmental organisations.
- The research also purposes to develop an appropriate methodology that will be significant in delivering the required study findings. The research will employ the post-positivism philosophy that is a revised account of the positivism philosophy. The researcher has also selected to employ the descriptive research design. It is seen that the research question is used to gain detailed knowledge regarding the IT and corporate governance structures so that their impact is applied successfully.
- The research will also present the findings achieved from the study and also provide a detailed discussion of the findings. The findings will critically analyse the relationship between IT governance and the enterprise governance of information systems. The results of the study will also deliver the impacts of IT governance, as well as, the factors required in implementing successful IT governance in intergovernmental organisations.
- Lastly, the research will focus on providing a summary of the study. The last section will also provide recommendations on the best approaches to transforming IT governance to enterprise governance of information systems.

This study is expected to portray the achievement of IT through governance to enhance the standard of the services in the public sector. The review will likewise depict how the corporate administration can help any organisation to accomplish their corporate governance strategy.

The research will, along these lines, shed light on the accomplishment of IT in various fields of intergovernmental organisations. This exploration predominantly portrays how IT governance can assist with developing their desired corporate structure. The study additionally puts the focus on the holes effectively recognised by previous researchers that concentrated comparable points.

1.3 Research Approach

The research will utilise a post-positivism research philosophy, which employs unbiased truth in drawing the objectives of the study. As such, the researcher will use the deductive research approach that depends on reputable secondary data that can unearth the problem of the study. The deductive research approach will enable the study to employ findings offered by the previous research so as to provide the required findings. The study will also be carried out using a descriptive research design, which is relevant in exploring different information so as to deliver the expected objectives. The descriptive research design will also allow the study to assume a qualitative research methodology that is vital in employing the available secondary data so as to meet the aims of the research. (Denzin & Lincoln; 2011) It is also important to acknowledge that the research will exploit the case study research strategy using a chosen organisation that will form the basis of supplying the required primary data of the study. The case study will be important in encompassing the adopted primary data with the accessible secondary data so as to accomplish the stated research objectives.

1.4 Justification for the Study and Role in Information Systems

In diverse intergovernmental organisations, IT becomes key to enable the organisation to provide satisfactory and better services to the peoples of any country. As stated by Armitage et al. (2010, p.76), "IT governance has come to the front of leadership in the public sector to generate IT value". Ndwiga (2016, p13) acknowledges that "To implement IT/IS in an organisation careful planning is required. There are several tools which can provide a partial solution to the management system of any governmental body. Frameworks such as ITIL, Prince2 and ASL would be applicable, but they cannot articulate 360° strategic issues. Therefore, to increase the flexibility and improve customer experience, a combination of tools need to be applied. As stated by Rhodes (2011, p.86), 'for every organisation, corporate governance is important' as it helps any organisation to increase the accountability. IT governance offers effective control and tactical planning in the organisation. The fundamental drive of IT governance in any organisation is to guarantee the IT applications alongside the dedicated infrastructure will be utilised fittingly by settling on the decision makers' mind of the position of their approach related chains to value expansion. However, the main issue that affects IT Governance is the initial implementation of the framework and generating an effective team to make the execution successful." (Ndwiga, 2016)

As per Pollitt and Bouckaert (2011, p. 49), Enterprise IT/IS administration recommends the needs of partners for responsibility and straightforwardness. At the point when corporate governance is connected, it shields the relationship between various administration groups of the government body. The expanded use of IT is the corporate structures and the expanded mindfulness in its level of significance in operations administration fortifies undertaking governance of IT/IS frameworks. As noted in the research proposal by Ndwiga (2016, p.13), "There are different measurements of ITG as noted by Wilkin and Chenhall (2010), incorporate key alignment between authoritative objectives and necessities and IT results; administration of danger; worth conveyance; and estimation of execution. Distinctive evolving technologies each have their unique of concerns and governing hitches, but also has commonalities. The worries raised by numerous rising advancements go well past the well-being and natural dangers customarily secured by regulatory laws, to likewise incorporate tremendous moral, social, and monetary concerns, including protection, decency, proprietorship, and human improvement issues. Developing technologies, for example, nanotechnology, robotics or even computerised reasoning (AI) include an intricate blend of uses, dangers, advantages, vulnerabilities, partners, and open concerns. Therefore, no single element can ultimately represent any of these multidimensional applications of technology and strategies they deliver. A differing set of governance players, projects, instruments, and impacts apply to every type of innovation."

1.5 Dissertation Outline

The next stage of the research will involve the critical review of the literature, which will highlight different theoretical and empirical paradigms that relate to the topic of study. The literature review will deliver two broad constructs that provide a basis for the determination of the objectives of the study. The critical review of the literature will, therefore, utilise previous studies that have been undertaken in the study topic of the research. The following phase of the research is the methodology section, which describes the research approaches and techniques that will be employed in carrying out the study. The researcher seeks to employ the deductive research approach that exploits a case study strategy. The case study research strategy will be relevant in providing a descriptive e view of the problem of the study so as to accomplish the desirable objectives. The research will also involve the collection of primary and secondary data, which will be utilised in the provision of the study findings. The researcher seeks to apply the unstructured interview to collect the primary data of the study. The next section of the research will entail the evaluation and description of findings of the study after the execution of the chosen methodology. The findings will be designed to respond to the stated research objectives so as to ensure that the problem of the study is solved accordingly. The analysis of the research findings is also presented in the findings section to portray the results of the research process. The research will finalise with the delivery of the conclusion and recommendations of the study.

Chapter 2: Literature Review

2.1 Introduction

The literature review section will highlight the broad constructs of enterprise governance of information systems and IT governance as applied in intergovernmental organisations. As such, this will involve the delivery of different aspects of these constructs so as to provide the basis for the research. The impact of IT governance on the enterprise governance of IT will also be evaluated in the literature review to highlight the significance of these approaches to the performance of the intergovernmental organisations. Ndwiga (2016) defines IT Governance (ITG) as "the procedure by which companies try to guarantee that their interests in Information Technology encourage vital and strategic objectives." Ndwiga goes on to explain that "IT Governance is a subset of more extensive corporate administration, concentrating on the role played by IT within the company. A great deal of information with potential relevance to the optimisation of IT Governance and its delivery is currently being dropped on the floor in the research domain. The basic design of the IT governance in any organisation is dependent on the overall strategy of the organisation. Effective IT governance is always essential for any governmental agency to facilitate well-functioning capabilities of the organisation (Rahman, 2007). Therefore, to implement an effective IT framework in the organisation, an effective methodology is required. This study, yet another investigation on the subject, describes the utilisation of IT governance to examine any relationship between an organisation's IT Governance development level and its business execution. By utilising effective IT governance in an organisation, any business organisation can achieve their goals easily. It shows how of IT governance works towards the Success of Information Technology and how it improves the standards of the services in a public sector organisation." (Ndwiga 2016, p.5)

2.2 Research on IT Governance

Research into governance structures distinguishes technology as a key power on flexibility (Young et al. 2006). Ndwiga (2016) highlights that "There are innovations that that undercut beliefs of resilience and those that can improve it. Justifiably, IT governance literature seldom considers the foundations of technological revolution in any element. Other literature, however, highlights transitional management towards specialised frameworks that are considered a progression towards Enterprise IT governance. (Smith et al. 2005)"

ITG is progressively being incorporated, especially by larger organisations. A latest study by ISACA establishes that more than 70% percent of agencies with fewer than 500 (FTEs) and 85% of agencies with more 500 FTEs report that they have some form of ITG set up (ISACA 2011). The ISACA study reveals that general progress of ITG processes is still moderately low, particularly given that the review was self-reported.

2.2.1 IT Governance and HRM

The majority of organisations have not established the relationship between IT governance and HRM, which is viewed to be imperative for the success of IT governance. Studies highlight the need to provide clear cut policies for IT HR so as to improve the capabilities of the workforce (Black & Lynch, 2001, p. 438). The provision of relevant IT training to the workforce would be significant in enhancing the IT HR. The organisations also need to have an alignment of IT and the organisational processes and objectives. The HRM of the organisation must also establish ways of providing performance measurement of the IT HR so as to enhance the level of IT governance. It is also relevant for the HRM to ascertain that the IT workforce of the company has the required skills of taking part in various IT projects. Black & Lynch (2001) also highlight that the HRM must also consider outsourcing of IT HR when the organisation lacks the required skills of undertaking particular IT projects. The HRM of the organisation should also define the necessary IT service quality levels to support the development of effective IT governance.

2.2.2 IT Governance Costs

IT governance in organisation provides different costs that are involved in the establishment of the required IT projects. The IT governance costs differ depending on the span of operations in organisations. The costs of IT governance are mainly incurred through elements such as business analytics, outsourcing, and compliance (Peterson, 2004, p. 16). It is also believed that poor IT governance in an organisation can increase the amount of costs accrued by the organisation. Studies have demonstrated the need for organisations to undertake a cost benefit analysis so as to ensure that costs are effectively managed in IT governance. Peterson (2004) asserts that the provision of the cost benefit analysis also ascertains that the organisation has a significant return on investment (ROI) of the IT projects.

2.2.3 Components of IT governance for Public Sector Organisations

According to Rhodes (2011), "there are five main components in IT governance that can help any public sector organisation to achieve effectiveness in its operations.
1. strategic planning,
2. external level of accountability,
3. internal controls,
4. objective setting and
5. supervision (internally and Externally)"

2.2.4 Five dimensional IT governance framework

Marwaha & Willmott, (2006) published in the McKinsey Quarterly Journal a breakdown of framework dimensions that are purported to drive value in IT through enterprise governance: this was also published by Hoch & Payan (2008)

1. The Leadership Mandate
Authority of the IT leader (CIO, CTO, etc.). Without the participation of the top-level management, it is practically impossible to manage the transformational program and the function in any public sector organisation. According to Biermann and Boas (2010, p.65), and Clapp, (2012, p.298). To enable any noteworthy transformation in an organisation, the leader must be on board.

2. The Organisational Structure

To balance the scale; incorporate organisational relationships that steer the business needs

3. The Decision Making Process

The composition of the project groups; identify, prioritise, and how IT meets this demand.

4. Mind-sets and Skills

As stated by Loorbach (2010, p.123), "in order to facilitate change in the organisation, different types of skills are required. Many governmental agencies handle the skill gap by acquiring partnerships with contractors; however, with time, the importance of the development of their own human resources is being realised gradually"

5. Performance Metrics and Incentives

KPIs must be defined to measure the progress of value on IT investment.

2.2.5 Sample Governance Tools applied in modern day IT Governance

The selection of an IT governance tool is mainly dependent on the capability the tool can provide to align the IT operations with the business needs of an organisation.

- ITIL: For service Delivery
- COBIT: "generally acceptable and applicable standard to facilitate the security and the control practices for the good information technology" (Ostrom, 2010, p.7).
- ASL: "one of the collections of best practices that provide guidance to manage the maintenance and development of applications" (Shleifer and Vishny, 2011, p.739).
- CMM: refine and develop the software development process
- Six sigma: As opined by Truscott (2010, p.318), six Sigma is the six standard deviation from the mean. It provides different types techniques that can improve the competency of any process and reduce the flaws by continual monitoring.
- Prince2: manages projects in controlled environments

2.3 Enterprise Governance of Information Systems

"It is generally concurred that norms give various advantages when accessible and applied. An Organisation's internal Information Systems (IS) management processes, in the accompanying instituted IS 'models', takes into consideration blending operations between organisation units, geographical areas and even distinctive service vendors." (Ndwiga, 2016). Be that as it may, numerous institutions do not have a composed procedure for characterising and overseeing internal IS norms, which causes vulnerabilities and postponements in basic leadership, planning, and design of processes and procedures. IT governance is one of these ideas that abruptly developed and turned into a vital issue in the management of Information Systems. A few organisations began with the usage of IT governance so as to accomplish a superior alignment amongst business and IT. (Ndwiga, 2016, p.6)

Next, many research processes are triangulated keeping in mind the end goal to see how organisations are actualizing IT governance practically speaking and to investigate the relationship between this usage and business/IT alignment. The real finding is that organisations with more developed IT governance are likely to acquire a higher level of business/IT alignment.

According to Ostrom (2010, p.8), corporate governance can be defined as "the set of practices and responsibilities that are mainly exercised by the management of any organisation with the goal to provide the strategic direction, and to ensure that the objectives set by the management can be achieved". On the other hand, IT governance can be defined as the "process by which any organisation can be ensured that they will achieve their organisational goals in an effective and efficient way by utilising IT resources" (Loorbach, 2010, p.167).

"There are a few critical measurements of ITG. Ostensibly the most imperative component of ITG is the configuration of decision making and hierarchical structures. What part do representing bodies, for example, the Board of Directors, play in the oversight and heading of IT? What parts and obligations regarding IT does the administering body expect and what is designated to senior and operational administration? How is IT to be organised inside the company? Is the procurement of IT to be midway composed inside a solitary, utilitarian IT hierarchical unit? Then again, maybe, is the procurement of IT to follow a distributed model to operational or managerial units inside the company? Application of IT Governance to services provided to the public is done by streamlining the processes and the operations of the internal governance structures." (Ndwiga,2016) Along with that, it also increases the collaboration with the public by generating effective channels for communication that can support both offline and online services for different state organisations and citizens (Loorbach, 2010, p.168). Furthermore, use of technology helps different organisations to re-use, combine, revolutionise and segment the technology to progress the effectiveness and the efficiency and reducing the excess related to any project. This, in turn, decreases the probabilities of any project failure. Integration is a significant element of enterprise governance on information systems. Different studies have portrayed that organisations can implement different approaches of integrating information system through the utilisation of enterprise governance so as to achieve the desirable objectives. Some of the approaches to integration include organisational integration and information system integration.

2.3.1 Organisational Integration

Organisational integration has been defined as the integration of information systems among different functional units and departments of an organisation. As such, different components of the organisation are unified so as to utilise a single system that can deliver according to the needs of the organisation (Agarwal, 2009, p.234). The different components integrated in the organisation include departments, people, technology, processes, and the functional units. The general perspective of the organisational integration, however, is highly determined by the supplier, customers or the manufacturers. The achieved organisational integration does not lead to homogenization of the components such that they lose their specialization; rather it involves different and complementary components working in unison without forming a single system (Melville, Kraemer & Gurbaxani, 2004, p. 286). The organisation can implement centralized or decentralized system integration depending on the nature of their operations. Centralized integration involves the provision of one focus of control for the organisation's information systems (Besley & Coate, 2003, p. 2614). The situation portrays that an organisation can have different servers around the world but they are all controlled from a single entity, particularly in the head office. The aim of centralized system integration is to enhance efficiency by utilising the economies of scale of the organisation (Besley & Coate, 2003, p. 2617). Centralized system integration was used since the early times and it propagates the development of system bureaucracy. The decentralized system integration, on the other hand, refers to a situation where the organisation distributes system controls to various parts of the entity. That means that for a global organisation, the information systems can be controlled from different locations where the organisation operates (Steinmetz & Wehrle, K., 2005, p. 10). Decentralization, therefore, breaks away from the traditional centralized system integration approach to avoid the bureaucracies that exist in the organisation. Studies portray that the decentralized system integration paves the way for the adoption of new IS/IT trends and also allows enhanced IT selection and configuration (Steinmetz & Wehrle, K., 2005, p. 12). Organisational integration can be internal or external. The integration performed with a firm is referred to as internal integration while the one that involves two or three independent firms integrating is called external integration (Mishra & Dhillon, 2006, p.32). Internal integration is further subdivided into functional and operational integration. Functional integration entails the integration of the support processes of the organisation. Operational integration, on the other hand, involves the unification of the primary processes of the organisation. Similarly, external operational integration is also subdivided into three categories, which include operational forward integration, backward integration, and lateral integration (Melville, Kraemer & Gurbaxani, 2004, p. 292). The operational forward integration entails the integration of the processes in retail and distribution departments of the independent firms. Backward integration, consequently, refers to the integration that is performed on supply processes of the independent organisations (Mishra & Dhillon, 2006, p.33). Lateral integration involves the integration of all the components of the independent organisations. The external functional integration comprises of the integration undertaken on the support processes of the independent organisations.

2.3.1.1 Powers of the CIO

The CIO of the organisation plays a significant role in determining the relevance of IS in the organisation. Traditionally, the CIO was mainly involved in the technical projects of the organisation; however, the role of the CIO has been changing with the increasing levels of innovation and globalisation. The current CIO is actively involved in the formulation of the organisational goals because the transmission and storage of electronic information has become extremely important for organisations (Weill & Ross, 2004). The CIO, therefore, has gained more strategic powers in the organisation such that the majority of the day to day IT functions are delegated to the deputy. Different organisations provide varying powers to the CIO depending on the nature of their operations. The majority of intergovernmental organisations, however, provide powers that relate to the development of IT and computer systems that support the planned organisational goals.

2.3.2 Information System Integration

Information system integration is viewed from a two-pronged integration process of the information systems. The first perspective is the technical approach, which highlights that integration is an instrument that portrays the interconnectedness of the information technologies of an organisation and the level at which the conceptual elements of data are shared (Agarwal, 2009, p.234). As such, integration implies to the extent in which different systems of the organisation are interconnected and also have the capability of communicating with each other. The second perspective depicts that integration is the level at which the systems of two or more organisations have standardized processes and the processes are joined together using computers and telecommunications technologies. Information system integration is undertaken to mainly to facilitate sharing of information within an organisation and the inter-organisation coordination as in the case of buyers and sellers so as to determine their capability in the supply chain (Hasselbring, 2000, p. 34). It is asserted that information system integration needs all application data, systems, and communications to be fully integrated so as to provide a consistent and real-time connectivity within functional components across the supply chain. The majority of the literature outlines that information system is not a source of value creation and sustainable performance for the organisation. However, integrating resources and aligning them to the organisational social and cultural context is relevant, particularly in operations coordination and developing workflows (Gunasekaran & Ngai, 2004, p.278). The past studies on information systems also demonstrate other types of integration that can be performed by the organisation. The strategic integration of the organisations information system ensures that the different integrated systems are supporting the organisation's core strategic plan.

As such, integration is not recognized as a goal itself, but just as an approach to facilitate the provision of the strategic direction desired by the organisation (Melville, Kraemer & Gurbaxani, 2004, p. 294). Communication networks integration is also undertaken by organisations whereby agents install integrated communications network by conveying around the world in visual forms, structured data, audio format, or text using flexible standards fibre, satellite, or cable. The electronic connectivity achieved between organisations plays a significant role in minimizing costs and enhancing efficiency and services through the tightened inter-relations. The organisations can also perform and coordinate internal activities efficiently to gain competitiveness. The flexible standards and connectivity play an essential role in supporting the communication network integration for the organisation (Gunasekaran & Ngai, 2004, p.282). There is one identified factor that affects the prompt responses of information systems, which is the absence of standardization for the main technologies that enable network connectivity. The other type of integration undertaken by organisations is data integration which focuses on the degree at which activities of different departments and business units in an organisation are constantly coordinated through the sharing of some several databases. This kind of system integration can be enhanced by the organisation through the improved standardization of data definitions and codes throughout the firm or in a larger scale that can include the entire industry (Papazafeiropoulou & Spanaki, 2015). The adoption of data integration in the organisation makes it certain that the users can only enter data once in various application components. Specification integration is also carried out by organisations and it involves the provision of specifications of the system technical design at the software, application, and hardware level of the stand-alone (Melville, Kraemer & Gurbaxani, 2004, p. 296). This kind of integration works well on the minimum specification of any information system, which requires minimum computer hardware. The highest level of integration that can be performed by an organisation is referred to as global integration. In the global integration, organisations go beyond the existing national and cultural borders of their location (Laudon & Laudon, 2004). The implementation of the global integration requires the organisation to consider various aspects that include politics, language differences, time differences, management styles, and customs. The global integration outlines three types of integration, which include cultural integration, international temporal integration, and international horizontal integration. This type of integration can be described just like a supply chain that goes beyond the geographical borders of the organisation, that is, a global supply chain.

2.3.3 Advantages of Integrated Systems

System integration presents different benefits to the organisation because of the effective systems established in the organisation. Firstly, integrated systems improve the performance of the organisation. The majority of the users of the integrated systems assert that the technologies perform excellently in meeting their expectations (Davies, Brady & Hobday, 2007, p. 185).

Secondly, system integration also provides high functionality of all in one solution, given that different aspects of the organisation can be integrated in single software. The situation portrays that the users have an efficient operating system that promotes the utilisation of the organisation.

Thirdly, system integration also delivers a balancing act among the organisational systems because different elements can be implemented in the systems altogether (Davies, Brady & Hobday, 2007, p. 187). For instance, the organisation can install updates to all the integrated systems at a single time, thus, saving time and resources for the organisation.

Fourthly, the integration of systems also promotes the provision of real time data because information can be sent to different systems at the same time. As such, the time lag that prevails between interfaces is removed by the implementation of system integration.

Fifthly, the organisation can undertake easier analysis of its operation because of system integration. Different aspects of the organisation can be analysed in an efficient approach using the integrated systems (Davies, Brady & Hobday, 2007, p. 191).

Sixthly, the organisation also saves costs through system integration because it runs like a single system that can be managed in an effective manner.

Lastly, the implementation of system integration offers efficient administration in the organisation because the administrator governs an integrated system. The situation portrays that maintenance, troubleshooting, and other aspects of the system are managed easily.

2.4 Impact of IT Governance on the Enterprise Information Systems

IT governance results in various impacts on the enterprise information systems because of the efficiency that is achieved on the organisation's information systems. One of the impacts of IT governance is the improvement of the firm performance because organisations that assume IT governance have a competitive advantage in the technology decision-making and in the minimization of operational costs (Van Grembergen, 2007). Studies portray that IT governance is a fundamental aspect of the organisation's corporate governance and its structures and process, which enable both IT and business to perform their duties in an approach that enhances the IT business value of an organisation (Liang et al 2011). The IT governance of the organisation has a significant role in eliminating the internal control weaknesses that prevail in a firm, thus, supporting the increased organisational performance. The effective utilisation of IT governance distinguishes the firm's unique assets when using IT, and also ensuring agreement to company's vision, mission, and principles. The situation portrays that organisations that have valuable implementation of IT governance can uphold unique assets of human IT resources, IT-enabled resources, and IT processes, which can enhance the competitive advantage of the firm, therefore, enabling an improvement in the performance (Papazafeiropoulou & Spanaki, 2015). It is also believed that firms with efficient leadership IT background have opportunities of developing their IT-related resources so as to improve the IT value of the business. The situation, thus, depicts that the establishment of the right IT leadership has a relevant duty in ensuring that IT governance can increase the firm performance. Studies also portray that effective IT governance can lead to enhanced IT capability in the organisation. IT capability is defined as the capacity of the organisation to deploy and mobilize IT-based resources together with the other resources of the organisation. The nature of IT capability is dependent on the IT governance undertaken by the organisation, particularly in the utilisation of IT investments and other resources in innovative approaches to create intangible assets and competitive advantage. Some of the intangible assets that can be derived from the increased IT capability of the organisation include knowledge-based assets, synergy, managerial and technical skills, and customer orientation. These intangible assets have been identified as key aspects of driving the competitive advantage of the organisation. IT users and organisational are more concerned with the ability of the employed IT investments in creating intangible resources such as increased business value, sales, and markets for the firms (Liang et al 2011). Based on the resource-based view (RBV) theory, the firm's IT capability should be rare, non-substitutable, inimitable, and valuable. Organisations that achieve superior IT capability after the adoption of efficient IT governance have stronger human IT resources, effective intangible IT-enabled resources, and compatible IT infrastructure. The provision of these unique resources in the organisation translates into an increased performance of the organisation. Lastly, the achieved IT governance of the organisation also has a significant impact on the improvement of innovation in its business (Papazafeiropoulou & Spanaki, 2015). The establishment of IT governance processes and structures improves the efficiency of the IT-based tools, which, consequently, enhance employee-driven innovation because they support dissemination, exploitation, and acquisition of knowledge. The aspect of information and knowledge sharing is highly associated with innovation, and should be stimulated by the executive management. The impacts of IT governance on the organisation's information systems, thus, have a positive influence on the performance and growth of the organisations.

2.5 Summary of Literature Review

The literature review was on the success of IT and how IT can be used in the corporate governance of any public sector organisation. The enterprise governance of information systems has depicted how integration can be applied by organisations in gaining competitive advantage on the market. As such, different types of integration can be adopted by the organisation depending on the intended results of the system. In the world today, you can hardly conduct Research and Development, Human resource planning, or even Business development without depending on IT/IS. Ndwiga (2016) finds that "implementation of the IT governance in organisation can provide a range of facilities to the organisation by improving their service capabilities. Along with that, it also mitigates different strategic issues in the organisation." Carr (2003) in his contentious critique *IT doesn't matter* makes a hypothesis that "IT's potency and ubiquity have increased, so too has its strategic value" He goes on to state that this assumption is "...mistaken. What makes a resource truly strategic—what gives it the capacity to be the basis for a sustained competitive advantage—is not ubiquity but scarcity. You only gain an edge over rivals by having or doing something that they can't have or do." (p.42) The literature review has also outlined the impact of IT governance on the enterprise governance of the information systems in organisations. Some of the major impacts highlighted by the past studies include the improvement of performance through IT governance, enhancement of IT capabilities, and the delivery of IT-based assets that promote the operations of the organisation. The implementation of IT governance has also been found to have the impact of improving innovation in the organisation, which also increases the competitive advantage of the organisation. The next chapter of the research is the methodology section that will outline the chosen research process that was used by the researcher in identifying the findings of the study.

Chapter 3: Research Methods and Methodology

3.1 Introduction

The research methodology will depict the process of researcher embarked by the researcher in the quest to provide the required findings of the study. As such, the research methodology will highlight the research design, which are the approaches assumed in undertaking the research process. The sample size and selection is also detailed in the methodology section. The instruments of data collection and the approaches to the analysis of the findings are also specified in this chapter. At this juncture, the researcher also highlights the reliability and validity of the research, as well as, the challenges and the ethical consideration of the research.

3.2 Research Design

The research methodology will depict the process of researcher embarked by the researcher in the quest to provide the required findings of the study. As such, the research methodology will highlight the research design, which are the approaches assumed in undertaking the research process. The sample size and selection is also detailed in the methodology section. The instruments of data collection and the approaches to the analysis of the findings are also specified in this chapter. At this juncture, the researcher also highlights the reliability and validity of the research, as well as, the challenges and the ethical consideration of the research.

The research will apply the post-positivism philosophy that is an adapted version of the positivism philosophy. According to Ndwiga (2016) "The aim of the positivism philosophy is to conduct superior analysis of different factors regarding the research topic. The main reason behind the selection of this research philosophy is this research requires different indisputable information regarding the topic of the research (Freshwater, 2011, p.113). This research requires the utilisation of different tools of IT governance and a comprehensive impact analysis of the IT governance and corporate governance using Different scientific figures and facts regarding the research topic." The post-positivism philosophy has numerous benefits that include the provision of detailed analysis and an impact analysis of the study topic.

According to Knox (2014, p.120), "this kind of research philosophy is intended to collect primary data". Ndwiga (2016, p17) notes that "the researcher did not choose the realism and the interpretivist philosophies because the interpretivism philosophy deals with different types of fundamental considerations and the realism philosophy deals with different real phenomenon that are not required in this research." She continues to say that (Ndwiga, 2016 p.18) "The research will also apply a deductive research approach because it "satisfies all of the research related questions by gathering different primary data and comparing it with the secondary information" (Morgan, 2013, p.55). It ensures a truth in the conclusions." "The main advantage of the deductive research approach is gaining higher degree of reliability and the certainty in the information. The main weakness of the deductive research approach is that it relies heavily on the initial premise of truth. Therefore, if it was concluded incorrectly then not only the deductive research approach but the overall process may fail. It collects primary information and checks the validity of the data by comparing it with the secondary hypothesis to gain accurate and valid information." Ndwiga, 2016 p.18). In this research, the researcher did not utilise the inductive research approach because it is "associated with the development of new theory or model that is not required in this research project" (Riege, 2011, p.80). Moreover, the inductive research approach is not logically valid hence not appropriate requires validated data. The researcher has selected to utilise the descriptive research design. It is seen that the research question is used to gain detailed knowledge regarding the IT and corporate governance structures so that their impact of applied effectively (Burns *et al*. 2011, p.65). It helps the researcher to answer all research questions, by describing the elements of research effectively and it also fill the gaps between to extend the understanding of the research. In order to satisfy the research related questions, it is important to conduct both the quantitative and qualitative research. As mentioned by Freshwater (2011, p.140), descriptive research design "provides an opportunity to get all of the answers regarding the research based question". There are several weaknesses associated with the descriptive research design. It may not provide the required level of confidentiality as it entails engaging in detail. This may cause huge ethical issues. Moreover, there may be some biases in the collected data that may present an extreme level of difficulty to resolve the problem (Morgan, 2013, p.320). Throughout this research design the researcher can collect the primary data from different sample respondents regarding the pre-determined topic of the research." Ndwiga, 2016 p.19) The study will be based on a case study that highlights the desirable aspects of the study, particularly an intergovernmental organisation that adopts effective enterprise governance of information systems. The case study gathers data to generate effective outcome but it mainly gathers data from a small number of individuals, or group so it cannot generate unbiased information, thus best suitable.

3.3 Sample Selection and Size

The sample selection of the research will be undertaken from an intergovernmental organisation that has constantly adopted effective IT governance and enterprise governance of its information systems. The chosen organisation will be significant in providing significant data regarding the impacts of proper IT governance and effective enterprise governance of information systems. The researcher seeks to utilise UNICEF Kenya for the sample selection of the study. The population of intergovernmental organisations in the world is not very high, thus, the employment of UNICEF Kenya will be relevant in providing the required study findings, particularly because UNICEF is a global organisation that has capability to represent the entire intergovernmental organisations in the world. The researcher exploits the judgemental sampling method, which is significant in providing an applicable sample for this particular study. The judgemental sampling approach enables the researcher to select the research respondents based on their capability in providing the required data of the study. The researcher deliberated on a sample size of 10 employees from the IT and information systems departments in UNICEF Kenya. The choice of a smaller sample was significant in ensuring that the analysis would provide accurate results that appropriately provided solutions to the study problem. The respondents from the IT and information systems department are well suited in the study because of their knowledge in the governance structures and processes implemented by the organisation.

3.3.1 Criteria of sample

- Ten (10) IT professionals in management level
- Head of department
- Sectional managers within IT department
- Benchmark Experience at 5 years. Sample covered the majority respondents with over 10 years

3.4 Mechanism

3.4.1 Data Collection Process

Cooper and Schindler (2010, p.75) insist that "data collection is very vital for an effective outcome from any research because it involves gathering different types of essential information". The research seeks to collect both primary and secondary data so as to offer sufficient data that can achieve the objectives of the study. The primary data of the study was collected through telephone interviews to the respondents between November 1st and 15th 2016. The adoption of the interview method was significant in ascertaining that the respondents would provide additional data for the research as opposed to questionnaires that deliver fixed data. The secondary data will form the majority of the data used in the research. To collect the secondary data, the researcher has utilised different valid sources from Scholar books, Journals, and online sources. For the data collection plan please consider Appendix C.

3.4.1.1 Ethical Issues during data collection

In order to conduct any research effectively, it is always important to follow ethics that protect the researcher and the sample respondents from any kind of ethical and legal liabilities. The researcher ensured that confidentiality of the respondents of the study was upheld so as to enhance the ethical consideration of the research. The researcher also sought the consent of the respondents before engaging them in the study. These two ethical viewpoints were considered as crucial by the researcher in the entire research process. Please consider Appendix D for the faculty's Ethics Approval Form.

3.4.2 Measurement

The utilisation of the telephone interviews as the primary data collection tool limits the amount of measurement undertaken for the instrument. The fact that the telephone interviews involve fewer questions also increases the limitation on the measurement of the instrument in data collection. The researcher developed the interview questions based on the topic of the study. However, the researcher measured the interview questions based on the type of questions addressed to the respondents of the study. The demographic and the technical aspects of the interview questions were highlighted by the researcher so as to outline the relevance of the data collection instrument. For instance, the first three questions of the interview were purely based on the demographics of the respondents of the study. The researcher felt that the distinction of the interview questions would be relevant in providing a definite measure for the study. The Likert scale was also used in some questions to provide valid responses from the respondents. The measurement provided by the Likert scale formulated in the study was aimed at providing the specific opinions of the respondent's regarding various interview questions. A sample of the scale used in the interviews is shown below.

Table 1: Sample Likert Scale Used in Interview Questions

Sample Likert Scale

Strongly Disagree	Disagree	Neither Agree nor Disagree	Agree	Strongly Agree
(1)	(2)	(3)	(4)	(5)

3.5 Investigation of Findings

As the researcher selects the post-positivism, deductive and descriptive research methodologies, it is very important for the researcher to conduct data analysis. The researcher utilised the interview questions in undertaking a qualitative and quantitative analysis for the data collected. A descriptive account of the findings of the study as linked to the available secondary data on the topic of study. A correlation study was identified by the researcher based on the responses offered by the participants of the research. The interviews will target the decision-making professionals in the IT and information systems departments of UNICEF Kenya, which is the intergovernmental organisation chosen for the study.

3.6 Validity and Reliability

The case study approach undertaken by the researcher will be relevant in using a real world case to explain the impacts of IT governance and enterprise governance of information systems on the organisation. The qualitative and quantitative research strategies are adequate in providing the solutions to the research problem because the impacts of IT governance and enterprise governance of information systems would require a comprehensive description of the phenomena, as well as, a valid explanation of the situation in the intergovernmental organisational context. As such, the outcomes of the study will be highly reliable going by the nature of the study topic.

3.7 Summary of Research Methodology

The research methodology chapter has highlighted various aspects of the research process that have been undertaken by the researcher in ensuring that the required findings are achieved effectively. The research utilises the post-positivism philosophy that is a modified version of the positivism philosophy. The researcher will also apply a deductive research approach because it enables the study to collect primary data, which can be compared to the available secondary data (Morgan, 2013, p.55). The researcher has also selected to utilise the descriptive research design. It is seen that the research question is "used to gain detailed knowledge regarding the IT and corporate governance structures so that their impact of applied effectively" (Burns et al. 2011, p.65). In order to satisfy the research related questions, the researcher find it important to conduct both the quantitative and qualitative research. The study will be based on a case study that highlights the desirable aspects of the study, particularly an intergovernmental organisation that adopts effective enterprise governance of information systems. The sample of the respondents will be selected from UNICEF Kenya, which is the chosen intergovernmental organisation that will be employed as a case study for the research. The researcher has chosen the non-probability judgemental sampling in identifying the sample size. The study will collect both primary and secondary data to provide the required research outcomes. The primary data of the study is collected through telephone interviews with the respondents of the study. The measurement of the nature of the interview questions is performed using the demographic features of the data and the technical questions provided to the respondents. The researcher also devised a Likert scale that was significant in measuring some of the respondent's opinions during the collection of data. The analysis of the findings will be carried out using the descriptive and correlational approaches, which encompasses both the qualitative analysis and quantitative analysis. The researcher reiterates that the study has a high validity and reliability, particularly because of the research strategies and approaches assumed for the study. The findings of the research will, thus, be applicable to the study topic. The methodology section has also presented some of the challenges faced by the researcher during the research process. The researcher has also highlighted the ethical considerations adopted in the research. The next chapter will involve the presentation of the findings of the research using the primary data collected from the sample and also using the available secondary data of the study topic. The presentation of findings shall follow two approaches, that is, the qualitative approach, which is a descriptive aspect of the findings of the study and a quantitative approach that enumerates the findings so as to deliver an appropriate correlation of the study variables.

Chapter 4: Findings

4.1 Introduction

The chapter will highlight the findings of the research regarding the objectives of the study. The findings of the study are delivered after conducting the research process, which provided significant data regarding the study topic. The researcher seeks to employ descriptive analysis in providing the findings of the study, which will exploit the secondary data of the study topic to deliver the findings that meet the set research objectives. The demographic characteristics of the respondents of the study will also be detailed in the descriptive findings so as to provide a picture of the respondents used in the study. The descriptive findings regarding the two constructs of the study will also be provided in this section. The correlational findings will also be presented in this section so as to provide the relationship between different variables to IT governance and enterprise governance of information systems.

4.2 Presentation of Findings

4.2.1 Demographic Characteristics of Sample size

4.2.1.1 Gender

The sample interviewed from UNICEF Kenya involved a group of mixed gender, however, makes were more than the females. The situation could be a portrayal of the male dominance in the IT field. The number of males interviewed in the research was 7 and the females were 3. The situation portrays that the organisation has 70 percent males in the IT and information systems department and only 30 percent are females.

4.2.1.2 Age

The age of the respondents of the study was between 25 and 40, but the majority of them were in between 30 and 40 years.

4.2.1.3 Occupation

All the respondents utilised in the study were IT professionals in the management levels. 9 of the respondents were managers in the IT and information systems departments while 1 of them was a head of department. The utilisation of the management level employees as the respondents of the study was significant in ensuring that the research would be furnished with expert opinions regarding the topic of IT governance and enterprise governance of information systems.

4.2.1.4   IT Experience

The majority of the respondents of the research had over 10 years of experience in the IT field. Precisely Seven (7) of the respondents had over 10 years of experience while the other three (3) had over 5 year of experience in the IT profession. The scenario demonstrates the suitability of the respondents in the research, given that they have earned experience that would be useful in providing the required information on IT governance and governance of information systems.

4.2.2 Descriptive Findings

4.2.2.1   Level of Systems Integration

The respondents of the study asserted that UNICEF Kenya has undertaken a global system integration, which implies that the organisation has unified its information systems across all of its organisations in different parts of the world. The circumstance is a portrayal of the commendable enterprise governance if information systems undertaken by the organisation. The knowledge of the level of system integration was significant in providing a broad approach in responding to the objectives of the study.

4.2.2.2   Effective IT Governance in Intergovernmental Organisations

- For IT governance to be effective in the intergovernmental organisations, there is a need for the organisations to view IT as a strategic business asset and also to manage it as significant portfolio. The adoption of this holistic view enables the organisations
- the intergovernmental organisations also discourage IT ignorance among the employees, and the IT staff contribute in technology investment resolutions (Zhang & Chulkov, 2011). The situation is imperative in ascertaining that the organisations can engage in IT investments that add business and social value to their operations. As such, they can easily succeed in the implementation of IT governance.

- in ensuring that IT governance is adopted successfully in the intergovernmental organisation, there is a need to have a vibrant IT executive and a board of director-level oversight (A.T Kearney Inc., 2008). The provision of these corporate level councils for IT in the organisations is prudent in ensuring that IT governance is aligned to the corporate strategy and also in measuring the level of performance of IT in different areas. The executives identified in controlling IT governance in the organisations have three main responsibilities, which include management of IT portfolios, ensuring IT and business continuity, and assessment and communication of IT governance.
- the organisations also undertake an IT governance model that responds to all the functional units across the world. The global integration of the majority of intergovernmental organisations makes it easy for them to utilise a centralized IT governance model that is adopted effectively (Zhang & Chulkov, 2011). In cases, where organisations have decentralized information systems, it is prudent to implement IT governance that is differentiated to meet all the functional areas of those organisations. Consequently, intergovernmental organisations must also recognize that IT is a vital aspect of corporate planning and strategy. The majority of these organisations have established formal IT governance structure that details the important of IT in the achievement of the strategy and corporate planning (A.T Kearney Inc., 2008).
- the success of the IT governance undertaken by the intergovernmental organisations is also determined by the level in which these organisations perform monitoring and measurement. As such, the IT executives in the organisations must engage in approaches that aim at measuring and monitoring IT capability in regards to the cost competitiveness and the quality. The execution of these success factors plays a relevant role in ensuring that intergovernmental organisations have valuable IT governance.

4.2.3 Correlation of Findings

Proposition Testing: Table 2 presents the correlation matrix, which is representing the relationships between the IT governance characteristics and the Success of IT governance characteristics.

The first proposition was designed to investigate the relationship between the organisational performance and IT infrastructure, IS projects, and system integration. The results depict that there is a strong relationship between the organisational performance and all the characteristics of IT governance. As such, it is an indication of the success of IT governance in enhancing the organisational performance of nongovernmental organisations in the world. The second proposition depicts that there is a stronger relationship between the innovation of the intergovernmental organisation and the IT infrastructure and IS projects. Consequently, the proposition also indicates the relationship between the innovation of intergovernmental organisations and system integration is not as strong compared to the other two IT governance characteristics. Despite, the difference it is relevant to point out that generally, the proposition suggests that there is a relationship between innovation of the organisation and the characteristics of IT governance. The third proposition examines the relationship between enhanced HRM and IT infrastructure, IS projects, and system integration. The results illustrate that there exists a relationship between enhanced HRM and the three characteristics of IT governance. The results displayed in the correlation matrix, therefore, imply that there is an underlying relationship between IT governance and the identified success impacts of IT governance, which validates the topic of study.

Table 2: Correlation Matrix for IT Governance Characteristics and Success of IT Governance Characteristics

Correlation Matrix

	IT Infrastructure	IS Projects	System Integration
Organisational Performance	1	1	1
Innovation	1	1	.8
Enhanced HRM	.7	.9	.9

4.3 Critical Discussion of Findings

4.3.1 Success of IT Governance

The majority of intergovernmental organisations have reported the significance of IT governance in their global operations. The findings of the research highlight that there are certain approaches that improve the effectiveness of IT governance, as well as, notable impacts to the global operations of the intergovernmental organisations.

4.3.2 Success of Enterprise Governance of Information Systems

The adoption of global integration among the intergovernmental organisations undertaking enterprise governance of information has been significant in delivering varied benefits that improve the performance of these organisations. As such, it has become significant for the intergovernmental organisations to stop viewing information systems as tools that provide support functions for the organisation, rather as important strategic mechanisms that would enhance their service delivery in the world. One of the major successes brought by the enterprise governance of information systems is the provision of enhanced strategic governance in the intergovernmental organisations. The global integration of information systems by the intergovernmental organisations has triggered the emergence of certain trends that have a positive impact on the strategic governance of these organisations (Agarwal, 2009). Some of the major trends observed after the efficient governance of information systems include flattened organisational hierarchies, strategic alliances, enhanced reliance on intellectual capital, the need to control an increasingly turbulent global environment, and the changing demographics. These emerging issues have necessitated intergovernmental organisations to introduce new information system competencies for the IS leaders in the organisations. These trends also call for the introduction of new competencies even to the non-IS employees of the organisation so as to foster the alignment of the organisations to the global information systems integration. As such, the mission of the IS function in the intergovernmental organisations is also changing from the focus in effectiveness and efficiency in a support role to a focus on organisational performance as the basis for a rapidly changing global market. In the majority of nongovernmental organisations, the information systems have become the backbone of products and service delivery, as well as, the client management. In this approach, the enterprise governance of information systems becomes a strategic partner for the performance of the organisations by being operational on a level similar to other main functions such as human resource and accounting. The change in the governance of IS in the intergovernmental organisations would result in the alteration of the roles of Chief Information Officer (CIO), which would be aligns the leadership roles of the CIO closely to those of the chief executive officers (Agarwal, 2009). The efficient management of the information systems in the intergovernmental organisations produces well engineered IS that promotes the performance of the organisations in the changing global markets. The second success portrayed by the enterprise governance of IS in the intergovernmental organisations is the fact that the changing global markets have resulted in a situation where the most creative and innovative employees have the key to organisational knowledge, hence, delivering a viable competitive advantage. In this case, the main impact created by the governance of IS is the improvement of the human resource management function of the intergovernmental organisation. IS has become a strategic partner for intergovernmental organisations to carry out decentralized HR functions initiatives. The utilisation of IS is significant in providing the solution for the majority of coordination issues that arise from the contracted human capital that is made to bear the organisational initiatives. The intergovernmental organisations have, therefore, identified the need to have the right HR and ARE staff that can collaborate to foster, encourage, and gaining cooperation between the parties involved in order to sustain effective and efficient compensation and staffing structures. IS has relevance in providing the required needs assessment that is related to the expertise of HR, and also in delivering the much needed technology-related training to the HR of the intergovernmental organisations (Agarwal, 2009). The intergovernmental organisations have also recognized the need to install advanced management information systems (MIS) that have the required business intelligence for improved decision-making in the organisation. Some of these organisations apply decision support systems (DSS) that enable them to make sound business decisions. The increased importance of IS to HRM will, thus, require the close association of the IS and HR staffs in the intergovernmental organisations. The findings of the research have demonstrated various success aspects of IT governance and the enterprise governance of information systems that prevail in the intergovernmental organisations. The enterprise governance of information systems and the effective IT governance undertaken by the intergovernmental organisations have resulted in a need for these organisations to stop focusing on IS and IT as supporting functions, rather to focus on them as key strategic tools of enhancing performance of the organisation. Papazafeiropoulou & Spanaki (2015) has depicted this finding by highlighting the need for organisations to have valuable IT governance, which can recognize the significance of IT in the achievement of the organisation's strategic objectives. The adoption of the enterprise governance of IS has enabled the intergovernmental organisations to achieve enhanced strategic governance of their operations. As such, the majority of the intergovernmental organisations are focusing on improving the leadership roles of the CIO so as to become closely related to those of the chief executive officer. As reported by Weill & Ross (2004), organisations should seek to improve the powers of the CIO so as to ensure that IT plays a relevant role in improving the performance. The enterprise governance of IS has also been significant in improving the HRM of the intergovernmental organisations. The integration of IS plays a vital role in assessing the performance of the human capital of the organisations and also in proving IT-related training that improve the service delivery of the employees of the organisation. The success of IT governance in the intergovernmental organisations is determined by various factors, which are considered to be relevant in shaping the IT governance model of the organisations. Some of these factors include the view of IT as a strategic tool and enabler of organisation effectiveness and competitiveness (Gunasekaran & Ngai, 2004, p.286). There is also a need for the organisations and the staffs to avoid IT ignorance as it can adversely affect the success of effective IT governance. The establishment of efficient IT governance in intergovernmental organisations has been imperative in supporting the achievement of the mission and goals of these organisations. The majority of the intergovernmental organisations have put much reliance on well-functioning IT governance for the sustainability of their performance (Carr, 2003). The situation is evidenced by the increasing costs of IT governance in the intergovernmental organisation. The findings have also portrayed that intergovernmental organisations also gain from IT governance through the enhancement of their business value. The implementation of efficient

IT government also enables the intergovernmental organisations in performing definite resolutions on the cross-cutting priorities and requirements at organisation-wide level on a rapid basis. Finally, IT governance has also been successful in improving the responsiveness of the staffs and managers of the organisations to IT as an enabler and a tool for enhancing the strategic performance of the organisations, which is relevant in advancing change management in those organisations. Papazafeiropoulou & Spanaki (2015) have also displayed the significance of IT in providing increased responsiveness for the management of the organisation because of the interconnectedness created by the IT systems in the organisation.

4.4 Summary of Findings;

4.4.1 Impact of Enterprise IT Governance

The world has experienced the increased change in the organisational context and also an ever increasing importance of IT. As such, it is has become difficult to imagine of an organisation that operates successfully in the 21st century without the adoption of dependable IT structures. The majority of the intergovernmental organisations outline that the role of IT has changed rapidly in the past decade from a back-office, supporting function to a significant function of a driving force and an enabler for the organisations (Mishra & Dhillon, 2006). As such, IT governance has become a valuable and dynamic asset of the organisation that facilitates the efficient attainment of its mission and goals. IT governance is also vital in managing knowledge and information, as well as, transactions that are necessary in sustaining and achieving the organisations goals and mandate (Gaines et al. 2012). The situation has made the majority of intergovernmental organisations to highly depend on well-functioning IT governance. The state of affairs has also resulted in increasing costs of IT among the intergovernmental organisations, for instance, UNICEF utilises between 4 and 7 percent of its annual budget on the improvement of IT infrastructure (Zhang & Chulkov, 2011). The stated costs of IT does not include some specific costs incurred on specific IT initiatives, which include information systems projects such as ERP, which might also employ the same costs as the one incurred by the IT infrastructure. The study findings also identify that IT governance also has an impact in the growth of the business value through the utilisation of IT. It is viewed that organisations with superior IT governance have a higher performance as compared to those that have not designed well-functioning IT governance structures. The implementation of effective IT governance is also observed as a critical success factor for prosperous ICT operations in the organisation. The effective IT governance ascertains that the ICT operations of the organisation are aligned to and also supports its mandate and strategies (Gaines et al. 2012). As such, the adopted IT governance mechanism should make sure that the decision-making process on IT strategy, investments, and directions are motivated by business to enable the close alignment of IT with the organisational business needs. The adoption of effective IT governance structures and process also enables the provision for the definite resolution of cross-cutting requirements and priorities at an organisation-wide level. However, the majority of intergovernmental organisations have challenges in implementing this aspect of IT governance because of their decentralized natures of their information systems. Another success impact of effective IT governance is based on its contribution to improved coherence and harmonization to IT project management methodologies, IT systems, and IT security levels (Mishra & Dhillon, 2006). Finally, the development of an adequate IT governance structure facilitates proper responsiveness of the strategic importance of IT among staff and managers, and also endorses IT as a strategic enabler and tool for enhancing organisational efficiency and effectiveness, as well as, expediting change management in the organisations.

4.4.2 Benefits of Enterprise IT Governance

IT governance provides various benefits to the organisation because of the enhanced utilisation of IT systems in the achievement of the organisational objectives.

1. IT governance helps greatly in aligning the organisational strategy and goals to the IT framework of the organisation. As such, the company can transform some of its strategic goals into IT projects that become achieved effectively.
2. the provision of IT governance also allows the organisation to have enhanced compliance, given that the governance structure would provide the required mechanisms of compliance (Peterson, 2004, p. 12). The situation portrays that the organisation would not incur additional compliance costs.
3. IT governance also assists in portfolio and project management of the organisation.

4. IT governance also enhances the adoption of IT strategic planning in the organisation (Peterson, 2004, p. 12).
5. the provision of IT governance helps the organisation to implement enhanced performance measurement.
6. IT governance also has the benefit of entrenching IT into the organisation's culture.

Chapter 5: Summary of Study

5.1 Contributions and Future Research and Development

The findings of the research have great relevance in being applied to both academic and practical situations. It is relevant to academics given that individuals studying strategic management and other aspects of international business can realize the importance of IT governance and enterprise governance of information systems. The circumstance will set new thoughts and understanding related to the importance of IT governance and IS in organisations according to academicians. The research also contributes to the business industry, particularly to the intergovernmental organisations and other international organisations that would gain significant knowledge on the need to have effective IT governance and enterprise governance of information systems. The policy makers in the industry will also learn more about the aspects of IT and IS governance that enhances the operations of businesses in the global markets.

Future research on the topic of IT governance and enterprise governance of IS can be performed by assuming a longitudinal approach that seeks to study the industry level of intergovernmental organisations. As such, the study would involve a research of over 20 IGO's so as to identify significant findings of the study topic. The other research that can be performed in the future is the study of the challenges faced by international organisations in the quest to adopt effective IT governance.

5.2 Limitations and Research Challenges

The research had a limitation of insufficient data collection because during the collection of data, the researcher faced problems in convincing the respondents. There was also a challenge in obtaining secondary information from updated resources. This is because organisations have come a long way and many of the published data on this topic are outdated, Cultural issues presented the highest challenge. While collecting information, the investigator worked diligently with the IT team. The data collection did not go flawlessly due to staff's attitudes to the researcher or the unassuming reason of an overcome crew that may have little time to speak or reply to the researcher due to work obligations. The research was also limited to only one intergovernmental organisation, given that the researcher utilised only UNICEF as the organisation of the study, which may not have been sufficient in portraying the situation with other intergovernmental organisations in the world.

Other Technical challenges may be faced. While the researcher may have not experienced issues like equipment and power failures or software and remote connectivity problems, there must be mitigation in place to counter an incident.

5.1 Summary of the Dissertation

The first chapter of the dissertation is the introduction, and it delivers the context of the research, which is based on IT success, that is achieved through approaches to IT governance and the enterprise governance of information systems. The general aims and the objectives of the study are also highlighted in this chapter. The general aims of the study are to investigate the influence of IT governance on the performance of intergovernmental organisations, and to evaluate how intergovernmental organisations can implement enterprise governance of information systems to enhance their output. The introductory chapter also outlines the methodology to be employed in performing the research which is a case study that employs both qualitative and quantitative research strategies. The rationale of the research is to study the success of IT by revealing how the utilisation of IT governance and enterprise governance on information systems influences the operations of the intergovernmental organisations.

The second chapter highlights the literature review of the research by highlighting two broad construct. The first construct is enterprise governance on information systems, which is revealed to provide various aspects of IS governance that relate to the intergovernmental organisations. The second construct is IT governance, which is also a broad concept of the research topic. The literature review chapter also highlights the impact of IT governance on the enterprise governance of IS.

The third chapter of the research is the methodology, which outlines the research method to be followed by the researcher in providing the findings of the study. The methodology chosen by the researcher is a based on a post-positivism philosophy. As such, the researcher utilises a case study research strategy that shall utilise qualitative and quantitative analysis methods. The selection of the sample of study is performed using the non-probability method of judgmental sampling. The researcher contemplates to employ a sample size of 10 respondents from UNICEF Kenya. The instrument to be used in the collection of primary data of the research is the phone interviews, which are generally unstructured interviews. The study will also collect secondary data from the available sources. The measurement of the instrument of primary data collection is done using a premeditated Likert scale and through the classification of interview questions as demographic and technical aspects. The analysis of findings is conducted through the descriptive analysis and the correlation analysis. The validity and reliability of the study is also highlighted in this section, as well as, the challenges and some of the ethical considerations of the research.

The fourth chapter of the research involves the presentation of the findings of the study. The descriptive analysis highlights that the enterprise governance of information systems and the effective IT governance undertaken by the intergovernmental organisations have resulted in a need for these organisations to stop focusing on IS and IT as supporting functions, rather to focus on them as key strategic tools of enhancing performance of the organisation. The adoption of the enterprise governance of IS has enabled the intergovernmental organisations to achieve enhanced strategic governance of their operations. Both IT governance and enterprise governance of IS are found to have successful influence on the operations of the intergovernmental organisations. The correlation analysis results depict that the there is a relationship between IT governance and the success impacts of IT governance in intergovernmental organisations.

References

Agarwal, K. N. (2009). The Impact of Information Systems on Organisations and Markets. In *Competition Forum* (Vol. 7, No. 1, p. 234). American Society for Competitiveness.

Armitage, D., Berkes, F., and Doubleday, N. (Eds.). (2010). *'Adaptive co-management: collaboration, learning, and multi-level governance'* UBC Press.

A.T Kearney Inc. (2008). The 7 Habits of Highly Effective IT Governance: Powerful Lessons in Transforming Business and Information Technology.

Besley, T. and Coate, S., 2003. Centralized versus decentralized provision of local public goods: a political economy approach. *Journal of public economics*, *87*(12), pp.2611-2637.

Biermann, F., and Boas, I. (2010). *'Preparing for a warmer world: Towards a global governance system to protect climate refugees'*. Global environmental politics, *10*(1), pp.60-88.

Black, S.E. and Lynch, L.M., 2001. How to compete: the impact of workplace practices and information technology on productivity. *Review of Economics and statistics*, *83*(3), pp.434-445.

Burns, R. B., Burns, R. and Burns, R. P. (2011) *'Business Research Methods and Statistics Using SPSS,'* 3rd. ed. London: Sage Publications.

Carr N. G. (2003). *'IT Doesn't Matter'*. Harvard Business Review. pp 41-49

Clapp, J. (2012). *'The privatization of global environmental governance: ISO 14000 and the developing world'*. Global Governance, *4*(3), pp.295-316.

Cooper, D. and Schindler, P. S. (2010) *'Business Research Methods,'* 11th ed. London: McGraw-Hill.

Crouch, C. and Pearce, J. (2012) *'Doing Research in Design'*, 2nd ed. London: Bloomsbury Publishing Plc.

Davies, A., Brady, T. and Hobday, M., 2007. Organizing for solutions: Systems seller vs. systems integrator. *Industrial marketing management*, *36*(2), pp.183-193.

Denzin, N. K. and Lincoln, Y. S. (2011) *'The SAGE Handbook of Qualitative Research.'* 4th ed. London: Sage Publications.

Ellis, T. and Levy, Y. (2012) *'Towards a guide for novice researchers on research methodology: Review and proposed methods'*, Issues in Informing Science and Information Technology, 6, 323-337.

Freshwater, D. (2011) *'Reading mixed methods research: contexts for criticism'*, Journal of Mixed Methods Research, 1(2), pp. 134-46.

Gaines, C., Hoover, D., Foxx, W., Matuszek, T., & Morrison, R. (2012). Information systems as a strategic partner in organisational performance. *Journal of Management and Marketing Research, 10, 1.*

Gunasekaran, A. and Ngai, E.W., 2004. Information systems in supply chain integration and management. *European Journal of Operational Research, 159(2),* pp.269-295.

Hasselbring, W., 2000. Information system integration. *Communications of the ACM, 43(6),* pp.32-38.

Héroux, S., & Fortin, A. (2016). The Influence of IT Governance, IT Competence and IT-Business Alignment on Innovation. *Cahier de recherche,* 04.

Hirst, P. (2013). *'Associative democracy: new forms of economic and social governance'*. John Wiley and Sons.

Hoch D and Payan M (2008) *'Establishing Good IT governance in the private sector'*, Transforming Government publication march 08 p.46-55 available at https://www.google.co.uk/url?sa=t&rct=j&q=&esrc=s&source=web&cd=1 &cad=rja&uact=8&ved=0ahUKEwj49fDv8d_NAhWHBsAKHWaoAWMQFggpMA A&url=http%3A%2F%2Fwww.mckinsey.com%2F~%2Fmedia%2FMcKinsey%2Fd otcom%2Fclient_service%2FPublic%2520Sector%2FPDFS%2FMcK%2520on%25 20Govt%2FIT%2FTG_it_governance.ashx&usg=AFQjCNGl_IvWa4VAZjKLFs3_ UBzMJSz0Cg&sig2=7_waB4I8yuUOkkcbT5lhbQ

ISACA. (2011). *'Global Status Report on the Governance of Enterprise IT (GEIT)— 2011'.* Rolling Meadows, IL: ISACA

Knox, K. (2014) *'A researchers' dilemma: Philosophical and methodological pluralism'* Electronic journal of business research methods, 2(2), pp. 119-128.

Larsen H.M., Pedersen M.K, and Andersen K.V *'IT Governance: Reviewing 17 IT Governance Tools and Analysing the Case of Novozymes A/S'* Proceedings of the 39th Hawaii International Conference on System Sciences available

at
https://www.computer.org/csdl/proceedings/hicss/2006/2507/08/25078
0195c.pdf

Laudon, K.C. and Laudon, J.P., 2004. Management information systems: managing the digital firm. *New Jersey, 8.*

Liang, T.P., Chiu, Y.C., Wu, S.P. and Straub, D., 2011. The Impact of IT Governance on Organisational Performance. In *AMCIS.*

Loorbach, D. (2010). *'Transition management for sustainable development: a prescriptive, complexity-based governance framework'.* Governance,*23*(1), pp.161-183.

Marwaha, S. & Willmott, P. (2006). *'Managing IT for scale, speed, and innovation'.* McKinsey Quarterly, 12(1), 14-21

Melville, N., Kraemer, K. and Gurbaxani, V., 2004. Review: Information technology and organisational performance: An integrative model of IT business value. *MIS quarterly, 28*(2), pp.283-322.

Mishra, S., & Dhillon, G. (2006). Information systems security governance research: a behavioral perspective. In *1st Annual Symposium on Information Assurance, Academic Track of 9th Annual NYS Cyber Security Conference* (pp. 27-35).

Morgan, D. L. (2013) *'Paradigms lost and pragmatism regained: methodological implications of combining qualitative and quantitative methods',* Journal of Mixed Methods Research, 1(1), pp. 48-76.

Ndwiga, C. (2016) 'A Research Proposal. IT Success; Moving from just IT Governance to Enterprise Governance of Information Systems in Inter-Governmental Organisations'. Unpublished Submission July 2016, University of Roehampton.

Ostrom, E. (2010). *'Beyond markets and states: polycentric governance of complex economic systems'.* Transnational Corporations Review, 2(2), pp.1-12.

Papazafeiropoulou, A., & Spanaki, K. (2015). Understanding governance, risk and compliance information systems (GRC IS): the experts view. *Information Systems Frontiers,* 1-13.

Peterson, R., 2004. Crafting information technology governance. *Information Systems Management, 21*(4), pp.7-22.

Pollitt, C., and Bouckaert, G. (2011). *'Public Management Reform: A comparative analysis-new public management, governance, and the Neo-Weberian state.'* Oxford University Press.

Rahman H. (2007) *'Developing Successful ICT Strategies: Competitive Advantages in a Global Knowledge-Driven Society: Competitive Advantages in a Global Knowledge-Driven Society'* IGI Global pp241

Rhodes, R. A. (2011). *'Understanding governance: Policy networks, governance, reflexivity and accountability'.* Open University Press.

Riege, A. M. (2011) *'Validity and reliability tests in case study research: a literature review with "hands-on" applications for each research phase'*, Qualitative Market Research: An International Journal, 6(2), pp.75-86.

Saunders, M. N., Lewis, P. and Thornhill, A. (2010) *'Research methods for business students'*, 5th ed. pp.52. Harlow: Prentice Hall

Scherer, A. G., and Palazzo, G. (2011). *'The new political role of business in a globalized world: A review of a new perspective on CSR and its implications for the firm, governance, and democracy'.* Journal of management studies, *48*(4), pp.899-931.

Shleifer, A., and Vishny, R. W. (2011). *A survey of corporate governance. The* journal of finance, *52*(2), pp.737-783.

Smith, A., A. Stirling, and F. Berkhout. (2005). *'The governance of sustainable sociotechnical transitions'.* Research Policy 34:1491-1510.

Smith, A., and A. Stirling. (2010). *'The politics of social-ecological resilience and sustainable socio-technical transitions'.* Ecology and Society 15(1): 11. [online] URL: http://www.ecologyandsociety.org/vol15/iss1/art11/

Steinmetz, R. and Wehrle, K., 2005. 2. What Is This "Peer-to-Peer" About? In *Peer-to-Peer Systems and Applications* (pp. 9-16). Springer Berlin Heidelberg.

Truscott, D. M., Smith, S., Thornton-Reid, F., Williams, B. and Matthews, M. (2010) *'A cross-disciplinary examination of the prevalence of mixed methods in educational research: 1995-2005'*, International Journal of Social Research Methodology, 13(4), pp. 317-28.

Van Grembergen W. (2007) *'Implementing Information Technology Governance: Models, Practices and Cases: Models, Practices and Cases'* IGI Global pp.(v)

Weill, P. and Ross, J.W., 2004. *IT governance: How top performers manage IT decision rights for superior results.* Harvard Business Press.

Wijsman T, Neelissen P and Wauters C (unpublished manuscript) '*IT governance in the public sector: 'top-priority' Available at* http://intosaiitaudit.org/muscat/Netherlands-IT_governance.pdf

Wilkin, C. L., and R. H. Chenhall. 2010. A review of IT governance: A taxonomy to inform accounting information systems. Journal of Information Systems 24 (2): 107-146

Williamson, O. E. (2013). '*Transaction-cost economics: the governance of contractual relations.*' The journal of law and economics, 22(2), pp.233-261.

Young, O., F. Berkhout, G. C. Gallopin, M. A. Janssen, E. Ostrom, and S. van der Leeuw. (2006). '*The globalization of social-ecological systems: an agenda for scientific research*'. Global Environmental Change 16:304-316.

Zhang, Y., & Chulkov, N. (2011). *Information and Communication Technology (ICT) Governance in the United Nations System Organisations* (JIU/REP/2011/9). Geneva: United Nations. Retrieved December 9, 2016, from https://www.unjiu.org/en/reports-notes/JIU Products/JIU_REP_2011_9_English.pdf.

Appendices

Appendix A – Questionnaire

1. What is your gender?

a) Male

b) Female

2. How old are you?

a. 18-29   b. 30-39   c. 40-55   d. 56-over

3. What is your occupation?

a) IT professional
b) Data analysts
c) Systems maintenance professional
d) Accountant

4. How many years of experience do you have?

a) 1-3 years

b) 4-9 years

c) 10-15 years

d) Over 16 years

5. What is your race?

a. White   b. Black   c. Hispanic   d Other   Specify: _____

6. Do you have a well-functioning IT governance system in the organisation?

a. Never   b. Rarely   c. Sometimes   d. Often   e. Always

7. Do you have an enterprise governance of information systems in the organisation?

a. Never   b. Rarely   c. Sometimes   d. Often   e. Always

8. How can you describe your IT infrastructure costs on an annual basis?

a. Very low   b. Low   c. Moderate   d. High   e. Very high

9. Do you think IT should be focused as a support function in the organisation?

a) Yes

b) No

10. Have you implemented systems integration in the organisation?

    a. Yes

    b. No

11. Which of the following system integrations has the organisation adopted?

    a. Strategic integration

    b. Global integration

    c. Specification integration

    d. Data integration

12. How can you rate the effectiveness of the system integration on success of organisation?

    a. Not effective

    b. Somewhat effective

    c. Effective

    d. Highly effective

13. What approach do you utilise when undertaking the organisations system integration?

    a. Centralized approach

    b. Decentralized approach

14. What can you say about the powers vested on the CIO of the organisation?

    a. Lower powers

    b. Normal powers

    c. High powers as CEO

    d. Does not exist

15. Please list some of the benefits accrued from the governance of the information systems by the organisation?

    a. _____

    b. _____

    c. _____

    d. _____

    e. _____

16. **Does the IT governance structure of the organisation have representation in the board of directors?**

   a. Yes

   b. No

17. **How many members belong to organisations IT governance are present in the board of directors?**

   a. None

   b. One

   c. Two

   d. Three

   e. Above three

18. **Which of the following elements do you think have been highly influenced or facilitated by the level of IT governance in the organisation?**

   a. Innovation

   b. Corporate planning

   c. Enhanced HRM

   d. Service delivery

   e. Organisational performance

19. **How often does the organisation involve the IT staff in the main decision-making process?**

   a. Never   b. Rarely   c. Sometimes   d. Often   e. Always

20. **Does IT governance influence the change management of the organisation?**

   a. Never   b. Rarely   c. Sometimes   d. Often   e. Always

Initials: _____   Time Started: _____

Time ended: _____

Appendix B - Interview Transcript

1) What is your gender?

2) What is your age?

3) What is your occupation?

4) How many years of experience do you have in IT?

5) Does the organisation have a well-functioning IT governance structure?

6) What is the level of system integration done by the organisation?

7) Please describe if IT is viewed as a support function or a main function in the organisation?

8) Does the organisation employ a centralized or decentralized approach to the IS integration process? Please describe

9) What are the advantages of system integration to the organisation?

10) What powers has the CIO of the organisation been accorded to support IT governance?

11) Does the organisation involve the IT staff in its decision-making process?

12) According to you, what are the overall benefits of IT governance to the organisation?

13) What cost does the organisation incur in undertaking its IT governance activities on an annual basis?

14) Does IT governance play a role in the improvement of the company's HRM? please explain

15) Does IT governance enhance the innovation achievements of the organisation? Please explain

Appendix C - Data Collection Plan

Main Activities/ Stages	Week 1-4	Week 5-9	Week 10-12	Week 13-15	Week 16-17	Week 18-20	Week 21-22	Week 23	Week 24-25	Week 26
Selecting the topic	■									
Designing the research proposal	■									
Formulating research methodology	■									
Collection of secondary data from other sources		■								
Discussing the literature review		■								
Submission and Approval of Research Proposal			■							
Review Research proposal				■						
Formulating interview transcript and design questionnaire					■					
Collection of primary data						■				
Analysing the collected data							■			
Document and compare findings								■		
Conclusion and recommendations									■	
Dissertation submission										■

YOUR KNOWLEDGE HAS VALUE

- We will publish your bachelor's and
  master's thesis, essays and papers

- Your own eBook and book -
  sold worldwide in all relevant shops

- Earn money with each sale

Upload your text at www.GRIN.com
and publish for free

www.ingramcontent.com/pod-product-compliance
Lightning Source LLC
LaVergne TN
LVHW042125070326
832902LV00036B/1065